3. CLIFTONWOOD

Explore
Bristol

EXPL◉REWALKS UK

ON FOOT

Julia Killingback and Michael Pascoe

Clifton Suspension Bridge

Taxi

Clifton Down Road

Clifton Village

	Start
	Cliftonwood Walk
	slope
	Viewpoint
	Steps
	Ferry
	Ferry Return Point
	Bus Stop
	Church
Taxi	**Taxi Rank**
	Public Phone Box
	Public Toilets
	Children's Playground

Clifton Hill

River Avon
← To the sea

Hotwells

1. CLIFTONWOOD

Explore
Bristol

EXPL◉REWALKS UK

ON FOOT

Map © Julia Killingback 2014

Cumberland Basin

At the half-way stage, the Mardyke ferry stop, you have several options:

1. Walking the circular route

Continue your circular Cliftonwood walk which includes a section along the open dockside. There are two long flights of steps which may not be suitable for very young children. Those with buggies may need help in lifting. However, there are also several long level stretches.

2. Return by ferry then bus

Take the ferry from the Mardyke ferry stop to Bristol city centre. The Mardyke is a request stop. Wave to the ferry operator – don't miss the boat! At the city centre catch a bus or taxi back up to Clifton. Ask for the Clifton Village bus stop where your walk began.

3. Return by bus only

Look at the Cliftonwood walk map. There is a bus stop on Hotwell Road near the Mardyke ferry. You can catch a bus from here directly up to Clifton. Ask for the Clifton Village bus stop. (Buses also go from this stop to the city centre where you can connect with other destinations)

Cliftonwood

Full Circular Walk
Total distance approx. 3 miles/4.75 kms
Average time needed – 2 ¼ hours

Downhill Walk Only
Total distance approx. 2½ miles/3.8 kms
Average time needed – 1 ½ hours

(Please allow time for ferry and bus connections.)
During the winter months ferry services are less frequent.
For details see Ferry Companies on page 43.

Our walk description begins at the Clifton Village Bus Stop
See the map pages 2 and 3.
This stop is close to the junction of Boyce's Avenue with Clifton Down Road, near the pedestrian crossing.
OS Explorer map 154, Sat Nav: Postcode BS8 4AF

Get there
By bus – From Temple Meads Station
           – From Bristol City Centre
           – From Bristol Bus Station (a nearby stop)
Ask for the Clifton Village Bus Stop.

By Open Top Bus This makes a circular tour of Bristol (from February to December). It stops at the Clifton Village stop.
Seasonal information: www.citysightseeingbristol.co.uk

By taxi – ask to be set down near the Clifton Village Bus Stop in Clifton Down Road.

Please note
This is a circular walk, so you may choose to begin at any point on our route knowing that you will return to the same spot eventually.

Mobility impaired   We are sorry that we cannot recommend this circular route due to the hilly terrain and some flights of steps. Enjoy instead our *Clifton* and *Victorian Clifton* routes.

This walk includes a children's playground. (🚸)

 THE QUIZ When you see a numbered question in the text STOP!
Look for the question at the bottom of the page. You should be able to discover
the answer from this spot. When you think you know it, turn over– the numbered
answers are shown at the bottom of the NEXT page. GOOD LUCK!

FUN FACTS. Look out for the smiley face
telling you more as you go along.

Welcome to Cliftonwood

As the name suggests, for many centuries the slopes below Clifton, down to the River Avon, were wooded. In the Middle Ages Cliftonwood was home to much wildlife and until stopped by their bishop, the monks of St Augustine's Abbey (now Bristol Cathedral) ran a pack of hounds here. Later the area provided much-needed timber for building both ships and houses. A vital industry developed – burning limestone – which was used for mortar, plaster, limewash paint and quick lime. Lime was also used as a disinfectant to make outdoor privies less smelly. For hundreds of years the majority of the local population lived along the banks of the River Avon, earning their living from shipbuilding, rope and sail-making, seafaring, and later, the manufacture of glass. In 1784 there were no fewer than 43 shipwrights and anchor smiths living by the waterside.

Gradually the population expanded and moved up the hill which has resulted in a delightful network of historic paths and steps leading to St Andrew's, Clifton's parish church. These are now mainly known only to locals. It was in the eighteenth century that several rich merchants built mansions on the upper

slopes of Cliftonwood to escape the squalor of the crowded city of Bristol below. One such family was the Goldneys who were shrewd investors. They bought an existing

▲ **Bristol from Clifton Wood** 1837
William James Müller

house in 1705, developing it into fine Goldney House. Gradually they acquired much of the surrounding slopes of Cliftonwood, then mainly woodland and a few smallholdings. The upper part of this estate became the Goldneys' magnificent gardens which still exist. It was the third Thomas Goldney (1696-1768) who did most to create the gardens which have attracted admiration from the eighteenth-century onwards. Interest in gardens grew as books were published and the Gentleman's Magazine which began in 1731 carried articles on practical gardening. Goldney's Garden Book with his notes still survives. Goldney and his gardener, Adam Sixsmith, who remained with him for 36 years, planned and developed the features which we still see today.

The house and gardens remained in the hands of the Goldneys until the middle of the nineteenth-century when the family started to sell off much of their land. The rapid development over the Cliftonwood hillside then began.

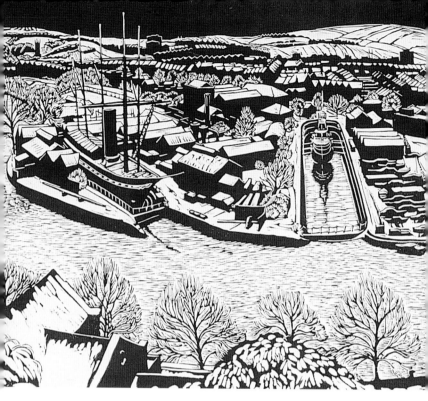

Much of Cliftonwood's history was shaped by the success of Bristol Docks over the centuries. First, trade was with south-western English ports, later with Ireland, then France, Spain and Portugal. The port was at its most profitable in the 1700s due to the notorious triangular slave trade. At this time Bristol became England's second largest city after London.

For centuries the River Avon was tidal here. When the tide went out, ships settled on the mud, sometimes breaking their backs. It is said that the phrase ship-shape and Bristol fashion referred to local vessels being built stronger than most to resist damage by such a strain. Others claim that the phrase is simply a tribute to the great skills of Bristolian ship builders over the centuries. Amongst the most beautiful craft built and launched here were the Bristol-built pilot cutters, sailing ships used out in the Bristol Channel to escort bigger vessels safely through the tricky approaches to the mouth of the river. It wasn't until 1809 that William Jessop (1745-1815) diverted the tidal River Avon to the far side of Spike Island and built a lock system in the Hotwells area which meant that a constant high water level throughout the harbour was maintained. As

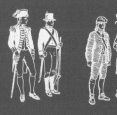

a result, ships could float safely all the time regardless of the state of the tide. Expansion of the quays meant more ships could be handled. Industries and businesses related to building and maintaining ships could prosper. As a result, rural

▲ **Bristol Docks from Clifton Wood in the snow 1995**
Trevor Haddrell

areas around Bristol became de-populated as more and more people were attracted to these new employment opportunities. This in turn gave a rise to a need for more housing to be built, which included the development of the steep slopes of Cliftonwood. These new houses were largely occupied by tradesmen, especially on the upper slopes. The census of 1851 shows sail-makers, policemen, gardeners and dressmakers amongst their occupants. Along the Hotwell Road by the harbour housing conditions were generally grim, severely overcrowded and insanitary. This resulted in frequent outbreaks of cholera and typhoid with far more cases there than in less-crowded Clifton higher up the hill.

In the 1970s the hillside terraced houses became desirable and affordable family houses, within easy walking distance of the city centre. Although Cliftonwood is not as well-known as Clifton, you will find it well worth exploring.

Facing the Clifton Village bus stop, walk left and cross the entrance of **Boyce's Avenue**, leaving the pedestrian crossing to your right. Walk down the left-hand pavement. On your left above you, you will see imposing Georgian Boyce's Buildings. This was the first-ever terrace to be built in upper Clifton in 1763. Thomas Boyce, a wigmaker, built it to serve as lodgings for visitors to the Hotwell spa situated at the foot of the Avon Gorge nearby. His monogram is on the pediment. Carefully cross the end of Merchants Road and walk down the left-hand side of **Regent Street**.

Once past the corner office buildings, look at the first shop on your left. It has kept its original Victorian windows. Pause here to admire the curved sweep of this brick-built street, dating from the 1870s and '80s. Look up right at the attic windows. The pediments are a prominent feature. Note the highly decorated cornices below the eaves. Pilasters and rather grand decoration flank the windows. Pause nearby the zebra crossing and look across the road.

● **Question 1** (*Look at the bottom of this page*).
Continue on the left hand side.

Look up right at the first-floor windows as you walk down the street. Each pair has an arched moulding decorated with different faces or motifs. Look for the pair, Numbers 9 and 9a opposite. ● **Question 2**

You will pass Saville Place. Continue along **Clifton Hill**.

 Look out for a mysterious door where no one goes in or out!

→ Stop when you reach the entrance to the grand house on your left. This was formerly *Clifton Court*, built in 1742 for Nehemiah Champion (1678-1747). Like other owners of several mansions in upper Clifton, he had moved up the hill to enjoy what was then open countryside, far from the densely packed city below. Champion owned copper and zinc works on the outskirts of Bristol and made use of the black slag (the waste product from his factory) in compressed form, to build

TURN OVER FOR ANSWERS	● **Question 1** What animal guards the shop at the far end of the zebra crossing?	● **Question 2** This building seems more important than the others. Why?

▲ **Clifton Court**
Completed c.1742
William Halfpenny
Architect

the upper right-hand wall of his house. You can see these bricks, known as Black Jacks, used in different ways throughout Bristol. Pause at Georgian *Prospect House* with its distinctive door surround. ● **Question 3** Following this is *Beresford House*. Both houses were built in 1765.

Pause by the magnificent ironwork gates and lamp, dating from 1822, at the entrance to *St Andrew's churchyard*. Two parish churches have stood here. You can read more about them in our Clifton walk. Continue along Clifton Hill, leaving the churchyard wall to your left.

To your right, below you, you will see the back of important *Goldney House*. Pause now to read about it. The second Thomas Goldney (1664-1731) bought an existing house here in 1705 and rebuilt it. Goldney was a Quaker merchant whose religion forbade violence. Nevertheless, he did invest in a privateering voyage. Such ships had an official licence allowing them to attack foreign vessels. In reality this made their owners legalised pirates. ● **Question 4**

● **Question 3**
Look at the garden of Prospect House. What makes it different from modern gardens?

● **Question 4**
What would you wear if you dressed up as a pirate?

Thomas Goldney's sailing ships, the Duke and Duchess, circumnavigated the world, bringing home valuable booty of gold, porcelain, silks and spices.

> When sailing off South America, Goldney's men rescued Alexander Selkirk, a castaway sailor, his strange story became famous through Daniel Defoe's book *Robinson Crusoe*.

Goldney donated two magnificent silver candlesticks to Bristol Cathedral in thanks to God for his success. Known by some as the *Robinson Crusoe* candlesticks, they can still be seen in the Cathedral's Lady Chapel today.

Now rich, Goldney's son, also Thomas (*1696-1768*), built a newly-fashionable orangery and created an impressive garden below his house. It has a formal canal, a raised terrace graced by a statue of Hercules, and a circular rotunda which overlooks the river below. Goldney also excavated a large underground grotto and furnished it with sculptures and a cascade. Its walls and roof are encrusted with exotic seashells brought back by his ships' crews as well as Bristol Diamonds (a form of local quartz) which shine out from the walls.

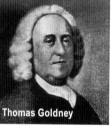

Thomas Goldney

Goldney Hall

The Goldney family intermarried with the Champion family of nearby *Clifton Court* (which you have just seen) and invested in Champion's copper and zinc works near Bristol. The Goldneys also invested in local ironworks that belonged to Abraham Darby (*1750-1791*) during the eighteenth century.

Originally wood was used as fuel to smelt iron. Attempts to use coal instead of wood failed because the sulphur content of coal made the resulting iron much too brittle to use. Darby moved from Bristol to Coalbrookdale in Shropshire where there were good supplies of both iron and coal. Here he found success by being the first to use coke (derived from coal) for smelting, resulting in stronger iron. As a result, Darby became a key figure in Britain's

Answer 1
Not a zebra, but a lion!

Answer 2
It is the only one in this row to have its name painted carefully on it in Victorian times.

Industrial Revolution. Goldney's original investment in Abraham Darby paid off handsomely for many years!

➜ Once you reach the curve of the churchyard wall, stop on the cobbles. The old steps and gateway close to you would have once been an entrance to the long-gone medieval church of St Andrew's. Looking downhill, you will see a tall tower through a gap between the buildings. Goldney had the tower built to house a steam engine. This pumped water to feed the cascade which still gushes through the extraordinary grotto below the gardens. In the nineteenth century the original Goldney House was greatly altered by Alfred Waterhouse (*1830-1905*) the designer of the Natural History Museum in London. It is now a University of Bristol hall of residence. The historic orangery, gardens and grotto are occasionally open to the public.

▲ **Coalbrookdale by night**
Philip de Loutherbourg, 1801

Answer 3
This is called a knot garden. You can design a colourful knot garden on squared paper when you get home. .

Answer 4
A knotted headscarf, an eye patch, earrings, a stripey shirt. and cropped trousers.

The Bishop's House

The fine building is the Bishop's House. Above the door is inscribed 1711, making this one of the earliest classical mansions in Clifton. The wings were added later. Look up at the urns on the balustrading. There is a plaque on the wall to the architect Sir George Oatley (1863-1950) who once lived here. He designed the University of Bristol's Wills Memorial Building with its landmark tower at the top of Park Street. This beautiful house became the Bishop's House after the Second World War, because the Bishop's former residence was destroyed by enemy action. It is now a private home.

➔ Walk on. Pause at the corner to look ahead at the old wooden sign **Clifton Road**. Before the use of cast-iron all road signs were painted on wood. Cross Clifton Road towards the T-shaped bollard. You are now close to *Richmond House*, the site of Clifton's original manor house, which was burnt down during the Civil War of 1642-1651. Rebuilt in 1703, it was once the home of a local merchant with the unusual name of Whitchurch Phippen. Note the two plaques by the door of Richmond House.

Pause for a while to look down at the rear of the grandest mansion, *Clifton Hill House,* on **Lower Clifton Hill**. This was the first Palladian villa in Clifton. The house was built for another wealthy merchant and linen draper, Paul Fisher (*1692-1762*) and dates from 1747. The architect was Isaac Ware who died in 1766. Ware was so pleased with his design that he included it in the book which he wrote on architecture. The monogram of Paul and Mary Fisher and the date are in the pediment. There are huge keystones over the lower windows and scroll brackets around the front door. Like many Clifton houses, the main façade faces south, away from you. The gardens, which are not open to the public, contain Tulip trees as old as the house itself.

During the 1800s Clifton Hill House was the home of the Symonds family. John Addington Symonds (*1840-1893*) poet, critic and historian was brought up here. The Symonds family became friends of the famous singer Jenny

● **Question 5**
Look above the door.
What animals decorate the
Fry family shield?

Lind (*1820-1887*), known as *The Swedish Nightingale*, and the poet and artist Edward Lear (*1812-1888*).

▲ **Clifton Hill House**
Completed *c.*1747
Isaac Ware, *Architect*

Do you know the poem *The Owl and the Pussycat*? Mr Lear wrote it especially for two-year old Janet Symonds who lived in this big house. Wasn't she lucky to live here and have a poem written for her?

Clifton Hill House became the University of Bristol's first hall of residence. Now turn sharp right down the diagonal footpath and cross Lower Clifton Hill. Continue right in the direction of *Goldney House*. You will pass the gothic-style porch of *Callendar House* (see the plaques) which adjoins Clifton Hill House. This was bought and later connected to Clifton Hill House to provide additional student accommodation. Pause to see the 1960s Fry wing to its right. ● **Question 5**

'The Owl and the Pussy Cat went to sea
in a beautiful pea-green boat;
They took some honey,
and plenty of money
Wrapped up in a five-pound note.'

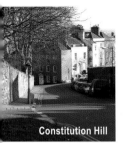

Constitution Hill

During the nineteenth century the Symonds of Clifton Hill House and the Fry families – who were then living across the road in *Goldney House* – became good friends. The Frys were benefactors of the University, which is why this last wing was named after them. The Fry family made their money from chocolate and cocoa and for many years Fry's was a major Bristol industry. ● **Question 6**

➜ Continue towards the triangle of grass. Turn left to walk down part of steep **Constitution Hill**. You will pass a charming Georgian house with the inscription *Clifton Hill Cottage 1715*. It resembles a classic children's dolls' house. The high wall by it surrounds Goldney House and its extensive gardens, all once part of forested Cliftonwood.

Clifton Hill Cottage

➜ Walk on down the hill. Pause opposite **Clifton Wood Road**. The early Georgian house, *Fairfield*, on the opposite corner was formerly a farmhouse dating from about 1726. Clifton Wood Road would then have been a rough track across the wooded hillside.

➜ Now cross to Clifton Wood Road. Walk along it close to the houses. Look at Number 2 with its gothic-style windows – the upper one is not real, but painted. It is said that a long-gone owner quarrelled so badly with his neighbour that he built this extension with the door facing sideways in order to avoid seeing him. Following two Georgian houses, you will pass a pair of late Victorian ones.

➜ Walk on. A little further along across the road you will see eighteenth-century stables once belonging to the mansion beyond them. Look left at Number 9 with its unusual Dutch gables and gothic windows. This cottage was originally built for a gardener at Goldney House. ● **Question 7**

Rather hidden, behind the wall to your right is the early mansion, *Clifton Wood House*, a speculative development dating from about 1721. It was designed by architect George Tully, for Robert Smith, a wealthy linen draper. There is an old gas lamp bracket over its imposing gateway.

Answer 5
Three horses.

▲ **Clifton Wood House**
Completed *c.*1721
George Tully
Architect

Look at the wall of Number 9. Can you see a badge? It's called a fire-mark. Today, if a house catches fire we call the fire service to put the fire out. In the old days house owners couldn't get help unless they had already paid money to an insurance company and showed their fire mark on the house. If a house caught fire, the company would send their own horse-drawn fire engine. Just imagine the poor horses struggling to pull a heavy fire engine up Cliftonwood's steep slopes!

Illustration by Basil T Blackwood for *Matilda* by Hilaire Belloc 1870-1953

● **Question 6**

Here's a sticky question! What is chocolate made from?

● **Question 7**

Can you guess the name of the insurance company for this house?

→ Now cross Glentworth Road. Pause to look left at the charming Cabot Tower on Brandon Hill. Walk on. Look left at the large Victorian houses. They have ironwork finials on the gables, ornamental bargeboards and unexpectedly decorative porches. Walk ahead along Clifton Wood Road, keeping left. You will pass Randall Road, then Church Lane on your right. Continue.

Look for a double bay-windowed house on your right, dating from about 1740. At some stage an extra front door was squeezed in when the house was divided in two! The last large house on the right, Number 28, is *Amherst*, dating from 1734. The style of the stone decoration around the front door is similar to that of Prospect House which you saw earlier.

The road narrows and slopes left. It is supported by a wall topped with copper slag blocks, probably a by-product of Champion's eighteenth-century copper works near Bristol.

😊 Find the name of the alley opposite you. What a surprise! Many years ago Bristol was just a small city. For people living there, coming to this wild and unfamiliar hillside may have felt like an expedition to the end of the world. Our walk won't take you there, but in the opposite direction!

→ Turn sharp right. This is **Southernhay**. Walk along **Cliftonwood Crescent** towards **Southernhay Crescent**. To the left, just beyond the modern houses, is a short un-named lane. Walk to the end of it for an extraordinary panoramic view. 🔆

→ Stop here to read to the bottom of page 21.

Spread out beneath you is Bristol's historic harbour. Its outline follows that of the meandering (but now diverted) River Avon's original course. On the far left you can just see the towers of Bristol Cathedral, founded in 1140. Right of the Cathedral (across the harbour), is the tall spire of the

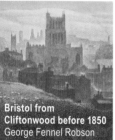

Amherst

Bristol from Cliftonwood before 1850
George Fennel Robson

fourteenth-century St Mary Redcliffe church and the square tower of St Paul's church, Southville, built in 1829.

Below you, moored safely on a sea of glass in the dock in which she was built, lies the steamship *ss Great Britain*. She was designed by Isambard Kingdom Brunel (1806-1859) and launched in 1843. She was then the largest ship ever built, twice the size of any other existing at that time, and the first- ever ocean-going, iron-hulled, screw-propelled vessel. Other innovations were her watertight bulkheads and iron rigging. She was engine-powered but also carried sails.

▲ *ss* **Great Britain**
Launched 1843
Designed by I K Brunel

● **Question 8**

Look at the enormous height of the masts of the ship. Her topmost yard would be at your eye-level if she sailed past the point at which you are now standing. It is no wonder that only the youngest and fittest sailors in the Royal Navy were trained to work at the top of the mast as upper yard men.

● **Question 8**

What does *ss* stand for?

Locked in *Punch*: 31 August 1844

The great feature of Bristol at the present moment is the Great Britain steamer, and it is likely to be a permanent feature too... for getting it out is quite out of the question, unless everything that surrounds it is utterly demolished. Brunel's calculations proved wrong. His new ship got stuck leaving the Floating Harbour and stonework had to be removed from the dockside before she could sail.

😊 Imagine sailing a stormy sea and being ordered to climb the rigging barefoot in violent wind and rain – 30 metres (100 feet) above the deck with the *ss Great Britain* rolling from side to side below you!

Brunel oversaw the building of his ship. Close by, around the docks, were timber yards for the masts and spars. In the 1840s and '50s Brunel probably stored his favourite Memel Yellow Pine here. He used this to build the many timber buildings and the amazing railway viaducts he designed.

Hillhouse's dock 1826

There were rope works and canvas sail-makers in the lofts. The sail lofts have now been replaced by luxury flats for people who rarely go to sea.

After sailing the world for almost half a century and covering over a million miles, the *ss Great Britain* was abandoned in the Falkland Islands where she was used as a wool store. A mere hulk, in 1970 she was rescued and towed on a pontoon the 9,000 miles from Port Stanley back to Bristol. You will get a closer look at the beautifully restored ship later on in this walk.

Below you, across the dock, there are still working shipyards, also a marina – the area is called *Spike Island* and is part of Hotwells. Beyond this, the River Avon now flows through the man-made *New Cut* on the far side of the island. Bedminster covers much of this area with Southville to the left and Ashton to the right.

Looking out over this dense housing, it is hard to imagine this as a once rural area with a population in 1801 of just over 3,000. A hundred years later it had grown to over 80,000. The area did not become part of Bristol until 1831. In the mid-nineteenth century Bedminster was rapidly transformed by coal-mining, paper-making, WD and HO Wills' tobacco factories, engineering and tanning. All these industries drew people away from working in the surrounding countryside to a better-paid, but far less healthy city life.

Answer 8
ss stands for Steam Ship.

To your right on Spike Island there is new housing on *Baltic Wharf*. Its name is a reminder that timber was once imported to these quays from the Baltic and Scandinavia.

▲ A square rigger passing Baltic Wharf c.1910

On your far right you will see two massive square brick buildings dating from the early 1900s. Known as bonded warehouses, these were originally used to store tobacco leaves brought to Bristol by sea from America. The leaves were kept here in bond before Customs duty was paid. It was reputed that every day a man on a bicycle delivered a cheque for £1 million to the Customs House in Queen Square. This paid the duty on the leaves and released them for cigarette and cigar manufacture. For many years this was one of Bristol's main industries. You will have a closer view of the bonded warehouses on our Hotwells walk.

I must go down to the seas again, to the lonely sea and the sky,
And all I ask is a tall ship and a star to steer her by,
And the wheel's kick and the wind's song and the white sails shaking,
And a grey mist on the sea's face, and a grey dawn breaking.

Extract from Sea Fever by John Masefield 1878-1967

➔ Return along the lane. The pretty 1734 house ahead (now watched over by a gargoyle) would have been the coach house to important Amherst above.

➔ Turn left and walk along the right-hand side of Clifton Wood Crescent, built for working-class families in the mid-nineteenth century. Reaching Church Lane, you will see The Lion pub opposite. It is over two-hundred years old.

➔ Cross the lane and continue past the pub into Argyle Place. Turn left immediately behind the pub, taking the path down. Here is the playground! 😊 😊 😊 😊 😊 😊 😊

After the playground, and a few steps down, there is an inviting bench overlooking the surprisingly green view of the city. Dundry church tower stands out on the distant hill. Continue down more steps to a charming leafy backwater. Look right at **Clifton Wood Terrace** with its interesting mix of old and new houses.

Old School Lane

➔ Turn left, towards a modern version of a Cliftonwood terrace called Old School Lane. It is built on the former site of the *Clifton National School*. Stop here to read about it. This church school opened in 1835 and catered for local children, teaching them the three Rs.

😃 Do you like working on a computer at school?
Children at this school lived long before computers were invented. The youngest only had old-fashioned slates, just like roof slates, to write on using slate pencils. Mistakes could be rubbed out with a damp cloth. Can you imagine doing your work on a slate?

A few years ago a 92 year-old lady, a former *Clifton National School* pupil, recalled that from their playground the girls and boys could look down and watch boys from a very different kind of school, the *Industrial School*, exercising in their yard below. The National girls threw romantic notes down to the boys who were poor. In turn these boys who had

Watch the birdies!

Estimates reckon that 600 herring gulls and 1,000 lesser black-backed gulls have found homes on city rooftops – probably thinking them similar to cliff tops. The herring gulls, are with us all year round, pilfering from rubbish sacks. Black-headed gulls visit in winter. Over 500 have been seen in central Bristol. They roost at Chew Valley Lake, but commute to Bristol to feed each day.

little to give away generously threw back their old socks rolled into balls. Despite the fact that these children were destined for very different kinds of lives at least this offered some light-hearted moments.

➡ Walk down the first group of **Church Steps**. After the railings pause to overlook the site (left) of the old Industrial School (now modern housing) and read about it.

The Clifton Industrial School, a Reformatory fronting Hotwell Road, opened in 1857 – to save lads from the streets when driven to them by the loss or misconduct of their parents, to give them a handicraft and to train them in honest principles. Some were sent here for begging or petty crime. Boys as young as 11 were detained until they were 16 and trained as brush-makers, shoemakers, carpenters and tailors. On leaving, many emigrated or joined the services. Continue down the pavings and steps.

▲ **Clifton National School** on skyline, and the **Industrial School** at road level. Illustated by Samuel Loxton c1905

▼ **Carpentry class at the Industrial School** by Samuel Loxton

Show a leg!

Did you know you can tell the difference between gulls by the colour of their legs lesser black-backed are yellow black-headed are red herring are pink

At the bottom you reach busy **Hotwell Road**. Pause here. Look across the road at the grand nineteenth century entrance to historic Poole's Wharf. In 1772 the Hillhouse family established a shipbuilding yard here. This continued until 1904, followed in the 1920s by ship repairing. Later, much needed coal was landed from South Wales and, more recently, sand dredgers based here plied the River Avon between Poole's Wharf and the sandbanks out in the Bristol Channel. The familiar quayside mountains of sand were destined for the building trade and road construction. The wharf was filled in and a housing development with an imposing new entrance built in the 1990s.

→ Walk to your right and cross Hotwell Road, using the controlled pedestrian crossing. Turn left to return along the far pavement. The *Mardyke* pub opposite dates from the seventeenth century. For centuries there were at least thirty pubs along this road which once welcomed in mariners returning from long sea voyages. Like other pubs on the Hotwell Road, the *Mardyke* offered lodgings for sailors on leave between voyages.

→ Turn right before the bus shelter. Pass the steps.Walk to the quayside ahead. (Please be aware of safety notices in this area). This is the *Mardyke*. Pause here to read on.

DANGER
DEEP WATER
NO EDGE
PROTECTION

The Mardyke was traditionally an area where ships could stand off when all berths in the city docks were occupied. When the quay was built and the road widened in 1860 local shipbuilders who previously launched their boats into this narrow stretch of harbour were understandably furious.

● **Question 9**

The Mardyke/Spike Island ferry started in 1845 and ran for over a hundred years.It carried an ever increasing number of workers to Charles Hill's shipyard and the timber yards opposite.With the arrival of vast container ships unable to navigate the *Avon Gorge*, docking instead at Avonmouth, and a rise in car ownership all six ferry services closed in the 1960s. Bristol docks finally closed to commercial shipping in 1975.

● **Question 9**
What do you think the giant-sized metal mushroom near you on the dockside can be used for?

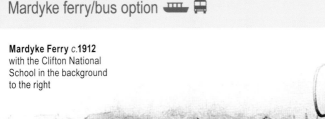
Mardyke Ferry *c.*1912
with the Clifton National
School in the background
to the right

Luckily for us, the ferries are back and we can enjoy the revitalised harbour from the water once again.

You can choose to end your Cliftonwood walk here if you wish. However the remainder of the walk is well worth continuing.

The next section includes two flights of steps where those with buggies may need help in lifting. It's not uphill all the way – much of the walk is easy and on the level, and it's full of historic interest and surprises.

O Mardyke ferry/bus Option. See the options on the map pages 2 and 3.

Fresh fish

Pike, bream, roach, eel are all found in the cleaner water of the docks, as cormorants have discovered for themselves.

The circular walk continues. Leaving the harbour to your right, walk to a nearby plinth.

This marks the mooring here for over 50 years of a once popular Bristol feature, HMS *Flying Fox*. She was launched in 1918, serving until 1973 as a training ship for the Royal Naval Volunteer Reserve. Training continues today on board another HMS *Flying Fox* in nearby Bedminster – a land-based centre, known in Naval terms as a *stone frigate*. The ship's bell hangs there now. (See their emblem below).

Before the *Flying Fox*, HMS *Daedalus* was the training ship here. In 1848 her captain and crew claimed to have spotted a huge sea serpent while sailing in the South Atlantic. The captain said it was about 30 metres (100 feet) long. To convince people he drew a picture of it which was published in London. Have you ever seen a monster?

Watch out for cormorants standing on the dockside. If their wings are spread wide, it is to dry them after fishing. A surprising variety of fish thrive here. In autumn you may see mute swans schooling their cygnets.

To your right across the harbour is the lively *Bristol Marina*. Sea-going vessels up to 21 metres (70 feet) can moor here. Smaller craft are able to navigate up-river and enter the Kennet and Avon Canal which connects to London.

→ Continue along the quay under a row of Plane trees. You will have a magnificent view of Brunel's *ss Great Britain*.

If you are lucky you may see other interesting ships moored here, perhaps the MV *Pride of Bristol* training vessel. During July Bristol pushes the boat out with an exciting and colourful Harbour festival.

Over 500 years ago John Cabot born in Venice, or perhaps Genoa (1450?-1500) commissioned the ship Matthew in Bristol. He set out in this small vessel to sail what was then

Answer 9
It's one of many mooring posts along the docks for big ships to tie up to. This one dates from 1904

known as the Sea of Darkness. Thinking that he would eventually reach China and rich spice lands, he instead landed in Newfoundland, thus making the first-ever recorded voyage to mainland America. (Christopher Columbus (1451-1506) reached only the outer islands, not the mainland.) This replica ship was built and launched in Bristol in 1997 and sailed to Newfoundland to re-enact Cabot's remarkable expedition of 500 years earlier. She is generally moored in the harbour but makes voyages during summer months.

▲ **The *Matthew***
This is a replica of John Cabot's ship built in 1997

Ahoy there! Look out for all sorts of boats – rowing boats, skiffs and canoes. Water skiers may skim by. Lucky you if you see the replica of Cabot's sailing ship Matthew glide past!

This Newfoundland stamp was printed in 1897 to commemorate the 400th anniversary of Cabot's voyage from Bristol - and his discovery of mainland America.

➔ Walk to the first modern waterside building ahead. You are on Porto Quay. Pause to look at the coat of arms on the sign board. The name reflects Bristol's long history of importing fine wines – especially from Oporto in Portugal. The city is famous for its *Bristol Milk* and *Bristol Cream* sherries. On a visit to Bristol the Prince of Wales, later King Edward VIII (*1894-1972*) after tasting a glass, said, *"If this is Bristol Milk you must have some damn fine cows!"* Until about fifty years ago it was quite common for Bristol pubs to sell schooners (large glasses) of sherry from the cask.

Bristol also imported wines from Bordeaux in France, as well as from Spain. Both Bordeaux and Oporto are twinned with Bristol. Walk on along the Quay.

The open area that you will reach shortly indicates a section of the *Lime Kiln Dock's* original outline. The dock was established in the early seventeenth century and was used for shipbuilding and repairs. Early road users nearby complained as the ships' bowsprits often impeded the carriageway. Lime Kiln Dock was finally filled in when the Canon's Marsh railway goods line was constructed along these quays in 1903. There is a bust of Samuel Plimsoll (*1824-1897*). You might like to take a seat beside him.

Samuel Plimsoll

● **Question 10**

Plimsoll, a Bristol man, pioneered compulsory marking on the hulls of merchant ships – the *Plimsoll Line*. For the first time it was immediately obvious when a ship was carrying too much cargo. This marking prevented unscrupulous owners from overloading their vessels in order to claim insurance if they sank. After several set-backs Plimsoll finally forced his idea through a reluctant Parliament and his line has been obligatory internationally ever since.

● **Question 11**

Believed to be Brunel's office

The Cross-Harbour ferry links with the ss Great Britain – now an award-winning visitor attraction and well worth a visit if you have the time – you will need plenty.

TF   Tropical Fresh Water
F   Fresh Water
T   Tropical Seawater
S   Summer Temperate Seawater
WNA   Winter North Atlantic

= Lloyds Register

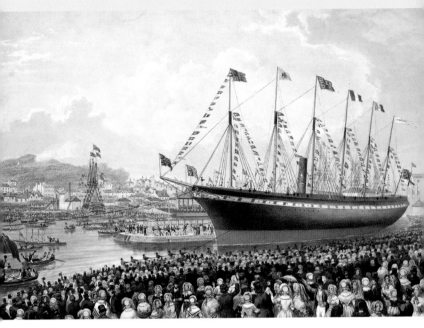

At the launch of the *ss Great Britain* Prince Albert, Queen Victoria's husband, gallantly asked Mrs Miles, whose husband gave a lot of money to build the ship, to perform the naming ceremony. (Newly named ships are showered with champagne – it's supposed to bring them good luck.) Her bottle missed the ship by a good 3 metres (10 feet) so Albert took over and scored a direct hit. Crowds of onlookers standing by cheered and the great ship got a real soaking!

▲ **The 1843 Launch of the Great Britain Steamship.** Joseph Walter 1783-1856 (print)

▼ **Maquette of sculpture on Paddington Station of I.K. Brunel** by John Doubleday (1947-)

After the launch, the Prince left Bristol by Brunel's newly-built *Great Western Railway* and arrived at Paddington, 2 hours 40 minutes later. He was impressed by the fact that he had made the round trip of 240 miles in 12 hours, including six hours in Bristol.

Stay on the quay to read on.

● **Question 10**

Have you got a toy ship? If you piled lots and lots of things on to the decks and let it sail, what would happen?

● **Question 11**

The tall wooden masts used to carry many sails. How many masts does the Great Britain have?

On a visit in 1724 Daniel Defoe (*1660-1731*) mentioned that Bristol had more glass-houses than London. In the eighteenth century at least sixteen kilns were producing glass for a variety of uses – you are close to the site of one of them. Many of the bottles were filled with Hotwell spa water and exported all over the world. The water was believed to retain its supposedly health-giving powers longer than any other bottled spa water. During the latter half of the eighteenth century Bristol gained its reputation for coloured glass, especially *Bristol Blue*. The kiln ceased production in the early 1830s. *Bristol Blue* glass is still made and sold locally.

Another important industry was once sited close to the dockside here. This was Bristol's first gas works. Bristol was not slow to adopt gas for the purposes of illumination. It is recorded that in 1817 it was used in some shops and for street lighting. Gas was first produced from whale oil and later coal. With the arrival of natural gas, the works closed in 1960.

➔ Retrace your steps along Porto quay.
You will see a long stretch of harbour with Underfall Yard, the tobacco bond buildings and Ashton Park beyond.

➔ Reaching Hotwell Road, turn right. After a while look left. You will catch a glimpse, between the buildings, of old Cliftonwood with its houses clinging to the steep hillside. There are five mature Plane trees on the roundabout. With their mottled bark and distinctive rounded fruit clusters, these trees thrive in cities throughout Europe.

➔ Cross the main road, via the controlled pedestrian crossing. Walk to your right along the pavement until you reach an opening on your left under the tall block of flats. Go under the archway. Pause here. ● **Question 12**

White Hart Steps are named after a pub which once stood here. Harts (wild deer) are long gone from this former wooded hill and today urban foxes forage in this built up area.

Answer 10
It would sink. Greedy ship owners allowed too many heavy goods on board. Mr Plimsoll's idea stopped this, saving many lives.

Answer 11
Six masts -- the crew called them Monday, Tuesday, Wednesday, Thursday, Friday and Saturday.

Before you climb, pause to look right at one of the two fire escapes on the ends of this block of flats – they resemble modern sculptures. To the right of the steps is an old cobbled gully, believed to be used as a slipway allowing strong men working with their donkeys to drag goods on sledges from the harbour up to Clifton above.

You will reach the delightfully-named *Cherry Garden* to your right. (You can take a well-earned break here.) As you leave the garden, look at the house opposite.

 Maybe the little window really is the Weeniest Window in the Whole Wide World!

▲ **Old Cottages off White Hart Steps**

● **Question 12**

Look at the mosaics!
What can you see?
How many of them are there?

Just before the path divides, look left at the corner house, *World's End House*. It is believed to have been the headquarters of Oliver Cromwell (1599-1658) when he besieged Bristol in 1645 during the Civil War. From this vantage point he would have been able to reconnoitre the Royalist fortifications on Brandon Hill across the valley. At this time, this part of Cliftonwood was outside Bristol's city boundaries and did not become a part of the city until 1835.

➜ Take the right-hand steps. You arrive in **Bellevue Crescent**. Once level with the street called *Bellevue Cottages*, turn around to enjoy the fine view over the cherry trees. You will see the city, the tall spire of *St Mary Redcliffe* church and, in the distance, the hills overlooking Bath.

➜ Take the left-hand pavement up the gentle sweep of Bellevue Crescent. It dates from about 1880. At Number 58 there is a comfortable carved wooden bench. ● **Question 13** Number 52 has an unexpected circular window and Number 40 has scrolls under its lintel. Continue past Glentworth Road and the more recent houses to your right. There's another bench ahead. ● **Question 14**

Take a seat to enjoy a pleasant view of *Brandon Hill* and the *Cabot Tower*. The tower was erected in 1897 to commemorate the 400th anniversary of Cabot's voyage.

You can see a building with round windows on the left at the bottom of steep **Constitution Hill**. In 1987, during alterations, an ancient spring called *Jacobs Wells* was discovered at the rear of it. The water bubbled up into a stone pool with steps leading down into it. Some faint Hebrew characters were inscribed into the stone lintel above the spring. The inscription was deciphered as *flowing water*. At first it was thought that this was a ritual Jewish purification bath for women. It is currently believed to have been used for washing the dead as there was a Jewish burial ground nearby. The building is now privately owned. The origin of the well's name is unknown. Its exact age is uncertain but it

Answer 12
Balloons!
There are 22 of them.

Away he (Sam Weller) walked,
up one street and down another,
only it's all uphill at Clifton.
The Pickwick Papers, pub. 1836
Charles Dickens

must pre-date 1290 when Jews were expelled from England for 350 years. In the Middle Ages Jews were forced to live outside the city limits and therefore settled in this area. They earned their livelihoods mainly by lending money at interest, a practice forbidden to Christians.

▲ The Cabot Tower from the Snake Path off Constitution Hill

Until recently there were only steep steps down to Constitution Hill below you. Now there is the swirling *Snake Path* built for everyone to enjoy, especially cyclists and buggy-pushers. It was designed and constructed by local residents with the backing of *Sustrans*, the national cycling network group which is based in Bristol.

 Why not give it a whirl on your bike one day?

Take the snake and **stop!** Then cross Constitution Hill to explore Bellevue opposite. Note the huge lion door knocker ahead!

Bellevue

● **Question 13**

Look at the unusual signpost in the garden here. One arm points to an unexpected place. What place?

● **Question 14**

Look out! There are creatures lurking under the bench. What are they?

The imposing terrace was begun in 1792 but was not completed until 1815. Look at Number 2 with its fine Georgian lamp bracket. Lord Lawrence (*1811-1879*) a popular Governor-General of India, and his brother Henry (*1806-1857*) who also soldiered in India, lived here when they were boys.

→ Walk up the terrace. You can see the original coal hole covers in the newly-restored pavement. Look out for another Georgian lamp holder. The grand houses face their historic communal pleasure gardens. Number 17B was once the vicarage of the long-gone *St Peter's* church at the bottom of Jacob's Wells Road. The house is the only one with a front extension, probably once a waiting room with a stained glass window. At Numbers 18 and 19 the fanlights are particularly delicate. ● **Question 15**

😊 These pretty windows over the front doors of Georgian houses are called fanlights because they are shaped like the fans used by ladies in those days.

Near you is a Victorian pillar box. Pause here to look across the valley at the castle-like building on Brandon Hill. This is *Queen Elizabeth's Hospital*, a school founded in 1586 by a charter of Queen Elizabeth I (*1533-1603*). The present building dates from 1843. (See their badge below right.)

😊 On special days the boys still wear traditional sixteenth century dress. Their uniform – a white linen neck band, a long blue coat with a leather belt, knee-length mustard-yellow stockings and shoes with buckles. How smart!

One of the school's former pupils was a pioneer of cinematography, William Friese-Greene (*1855-1921*).

→ Cross Lower Clifton Hill and walk down alongside the wall opposite. Continue to the gateway of a graveyard to your

Answer 13
Home.
There's no place like home.

Answer 14
Two snakes – mind they don't bite your ankles!

left and stop here. This is called the *Strangers' Burial Ground*. In the late 1700s many sick visitors who had come for a cure to the nearby Hotwell spa died. Local people complained because the large number of burials meant that they were being prevented from being buried with their ancestors in *St Andrew's churchyard* at the top of the hill. So, from 1787, this new graveyard was opened and the poor visiting victims were buried here, well away from the area's residents. It was extended later. The grave of the scientist Dr Beddoes (*1760-1808*) is here. You can read more about this unusual character in our Hotwells walk.

▲ **Strangers' Burial Ground**
Opened 1787, closed 1871

Close to you, on the other side of the road, you will see the colourful façade of *Hill's Almshouse*, opened in 1867, the gift of Thomas Hill. He was a notable philanthropist and, among many other gifts to the city, donated a wing to the *Bristol Royal Infirmary*. The almshouse was designed by Charles Hansom (*1817-1888*) who also designed *Clifton College*. It was originally built to house twelve worthy elderly women. Closer to you is their small almshouse chapel. ● **Question 16**

● **Question 15**

Look at Number 19. Why is there an arrow cut into the stone base of the wall by the garden gate?

● **Question 16**

Look! There's a stone animal on the roof of the chapel. What kind of animal is it?

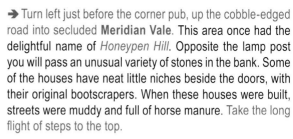

→ Turn left just before the corner pub, up the cobble-edged road into secluded **Meridian Vale**. This area once had the delightful name of *Honeypen Hill*. Opposite the lamp post you will pass an unusual variety of stones in the bank. Some of the houses have neat little niches beside the doors, with their original bootscrapers. When these houses were built, streets were muddy and full of horse manure. Take the long flight of steps to the top.

😃 As you climb you will see houses ahead of you, called *Dover Place Cottages*. Look how tall the buildings are. You can see six levels of windows on this side. When you get to the top count how many levels of windows there are on the street side. Not so many because the houses are built right into the cliff face of an old quarry.

Reaching the top, you are near the junction of Meridian Place and **Dover Place**. Look across the road at the fine Regency houses of the early 1800s with their attractive balconies. Turn left. Walk along the left-hand pavement of Dover Place. The houses, which date from the 1860s, are unusual with their heavy Tuscan-style windows, unusual worm-cast carved stone above them and trefoil features over the entrances. Look too at the different kinds of railings. Walk on. ● **Question 17**

😃 Older boys from wealthy families were usually sent away to boarding schools. Most girls were taught at home – music, embroidery and flower drawing. If they were taught at all, poorer children went to church or chapel schools and had to leave at an early age to start work.

→ Walk on just past the houses. You can now see across to Brandon Hill and look down over the lonely Strangers' Burial Ground. If you are lucky you might see a family of foxes which live undisturbed in this wild place. The large building to your right is *Manor Hall*, a University of Bristol hall of residence built in the 1930s.

Answer 15
This arrow called a benchmark shows how high this point is above sea level. Past mapmakers used these. Now satellites are used. Bristol, a city of seven hills was hard to map.

Answer 16
A lion.
He is holding a shield.

➜ Retrace your steps and cross to the far pavement of adjoining **Gordon Road**. Turn left down it. Following three large houses opposite, built in the 1830s, you pass an old converted coach house. Cross the end of Wetherall Place and look right. On the left, at the far end of the street, is a red-brick Gothic-style house which was once the home of Joseph Hansom (1803-1882) inventor of the Hansom cab and brother of Charles Hansom the architect of *Clifton College.* Find out more in our Victorian Clifton walk.

▲ Cabot Tower, Brandon Hill and Queen Elizabeth Hospital

➜ Continue. To your left, set back from the road is pretty Regency Grosvenor House. Cross the road here to see its imposing Gothic-style entrance. Next is a small terrace. At Number 23 there is a plaque dedicated to Annie Kenney (*1879-1953*). Annie, a working class suffragette, became a colleague of Emmeline Pankhurst (*1858-1928*) a leading suffragette who fought for women's right to vote. Annie was imprisoned thirteen times for her militancy. She lived here in 1910.

● **Question 17**

Stop at Number 11. Look at the writing painted close to the doorbell. There was a business here in the early 1900s. What was it?

Did you know?

Women received the vote on equal terms as men (both had to be over 21) when the Representation of the People Act was passed in 1928.

VOTES FOR WOMEN

You pass a pub. This is the site of the former *Richmond Spring*. Before mains water became available in the 1850s, together with the nearby *Buckingham Spring*, these provided vital fresh water for local residents. Walk on to the end of Gordon Road. Pause to look right at Buckingham Place with its pleasant first-floor balconies. It was built in 1845. Ahead is the impressive *Buckingham Baptist Chapel* built in 1847. The architect, R S Pope (1795-1884) is said to have generously donated his fee to pay for the decoration which is modelled on Sainte Chapelle in Paris. Visitors are welcome.

Pause to look at the Georgian lamp-holder at the top of the steps and see where the lamplighter once rested his ladder. Go left into Richmond Lane.

➔ Continue along the lane which runs parallel to Gordon Road. On your right you will catch a glimpse through a gate of the large communal garden belonging to 1790s **Richmond Terrace**. Unusually, this three-sided terrace was built around its gardens with their backs, rather than their fronts, overlooking them. ● **Question 18**

➔ Follow the pavement round and climb up the first steps on your right to walk along one side of Richmond Terrace. Like several other Clifton terraces it was built by William Paty (*1758-1800*). This first section has been restored by the University of Bristol for student accommodation. Walk along. Number 29 has a coloured bird flying in the fanlight. Number 26 also has pretty leaded glass. ● **Question 19**

➔ Walk on and turn the corner. Enjoy the view over Victorian *St Andrew's Churchyard*. Keep walking along the high pavement. Look out for the variety of attractive fanlights including at Number 20 – reminiscent of a spider's web. Number 17 has its original curved glass candle lamp over the door. It was obligatory in the days before street lighting to shed candle light both inside and outside the house.

 Look! There's a dolphin door knocker.

Answer 17

A Governess Agency Office. Rich parents could find governesses (private home teachers) for their younger children here.

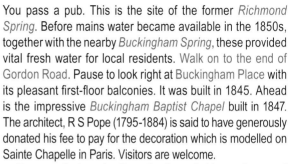

DOMESTIC SERVANTS' INSTITU-
TION, 11, DOVER PLACE.
This Institution is intended to provide Lodgings for respectable Servants while waiting for Situations, and a Registry is connected with it through which Families can be supplied with Servants. A Matron is in attendance every day, from 10 a.m. to 5 p.m., except on Saturdays, when attendance is only given till 2 p.m.
9541

Clifton Chronicle 1880

Several of the houses have been finished with rough stucco rather than stone. Using this cement render over walls made of rough stone and incising it to look like individual stone blocks, was obviously a much cheaper alternative to using dressed stone.

▲ **Richmond Terrace**
Commenced c.1790

➜ Go down the steps here. Cross the road towards a fountain, close to the entrance to the graveyard. The fountain probably dates from about 1850 and is similar to another by Bedminster Bridge, Bristol. The carved inscription in the stonework reads: *The fear of the Lord is a fountain of life. Prov.* The quotation is taken from the Bible – the Book of Proverbs, Chapter 14 Verse 27. The niche is surrounded by a rope design which reminds us of Bristol's seagoing history. There are shell motifs within the small niches below.

☺ Have a *pretend* drink! In Victorian times walkers could stop for a real drink of fresh water from lead cups attached by chains to this pretty fountain.

● **Question 18**

Just before the street turns right find a window with a leaf decoration above it. What can you spot which proves this was once a doorway?

● **Question 19**

Look at the railings at Number 25. What do they remind you of?

➔ Cross the Fosseway cul-de-sac. Pause to enjoy the view along Lansdown Place ahead dating from 1845.

Take the left-hand pavement past the 1865 hotel. Cross the busy main road via the pedestrian island. Go past the bollards to Bird Cage Walk, the footpath crossing *Victoria Square* gardens. In Victorian times the gardens were railed off for the private use of the wealthy residents, the "caged birds" of the square.

➔ Walk on. In the right-hand garden there is a fine old Cedar tree, one of many beautiful trees, some dating back 150 years. The right-hand terrace of Victoria Square was originally called *Royal Promenade* and dates from 1851. John Addington Symonds of Clifton Hill House, mentioned earlier, lived here for six years.

➔ Leaving the gardens behind, walk on towards the archway. Look at the terrace to your left with its magnificent ironwork. At Number 15 there is a plaque to the famous cricketer, Dr W.G.Grace (*1848-1915*) who captained England, Gloucestershire and other teams. Although he is known primarily as a batsman he was an all-rounder at cricket as well as being a champion hurdler and an excellent footballer and golfer. Grace is usually credited with inventing modern cricket. Before the arch, to your right, is the attractive detached early Victorian villa, called *Albert Lodge*, named after Prince Albert (*1819-1861*), the Consort of Queen Victoria (*1819-1901*). ● **Question 20**

➔ Go under the arch into **Boyce's Avenue**. You will see the Albion pub/restaurant to your left, and opposite the Victorian *Clifton Arcade.* Continue along Boyce's Avenue to **Clifton Down Road**. You are now close to the Clifton Village bus stop from which you began your walk. You can reward yourself with a well-deserved treat in one of Clifton's many cafés.

We hope that you enjoyed walking your Cliftonwood and Clifton Village round.

Answer 18

At foot level there is an alcove that once held a bootscraper for cleaning dirty boots. Wipe your feet please!

Answer 19

Tassels – they're made of cast-iron but they look real.

▲ **Bristol from the Docks** *c.*1807 - *detail.* William Westall.

It is hard to imagine that the now densely populated area of Cliftonwood was once just a peaceful wooded slope, filled with birdsong, or that today's leisure area of Bristol docks was crowded with sailing ships landing their varied and exotic cargoes from every continent. Picture a Cliftonwood forester taking time out to rest his tired back after once again stacking logs, looking down over the harbour, dreaming of sailing the seven seas. Imagine too a hardy sailor aboard a merchant ship below, ordered to cast off yet again, looking longingly up at the green slopes of Cliftonwood, wishing that he could make a far safer living ashore. Both, no doubt, would have thought how much sweeter their lives would be if they were ever to become as rich and successful as the wealthy merchant Mr Thomas Goldney, living in such splendour at the top of Clifton Wood hill.

● **Question 20**

Just before you reach the arch look up. Someone has their head carved in stone. Whose head is it?

The Authors

Julia Killingback

A long-term resident who has been much involved in projects promoting this beautiful area. Julia studied art in Bristol (NDD ATD) designing dress textiles in Paris before returning to Bristol to establish her own Studio. Her designs were used on varied products by well-known companies worldwide. Previous published work. Illustrations for 7 Littlest Poetry Books. Author and Illustrator of 12 children's books (Methuen).

Michael Pascoe

Michael Pascoe has made a DVD - "Clifton - a place for all seasons" produced by 1st-Take and a book "The Clifton Guide" published by Redcliffe Press as well as writing many articles on Clifton and Hotwells' rich history. More recently, he co-authored the official guide to the Clifton Suspension Bridge. In 2005 he was awarded the Lord Mayor's medal "for services to Bristol and Clifton".

Acknowledgements:

The authors are most grateful for the goodwill and generosity of the following in helping towards the preparation of this book:

Pippa Gibbs for her kind and attentive editing; Simon Bishop for his expertise in graphic design; Richard Bland's assistance with the flora and fauna and Dawn Dyer (Bristol City Reference Library) for her unfailing help.

Our thanks also go to Anthony Beeson, David Bolton, Simon Gibbs, Elfyn Griffith, Trevor Haddrell, Clara Hudson, Alison Lewis, Andy Lillie, Tom Mocek, Rose Mary Musgrave, Pim Palmen, John Parkes and Ray Smith.

The authors would especially like to thank the individuals, families, friends and children who kindly 'route tested' our walks in all winds and weathers – and approved them! Their comments were invaluable.

Credits

The authors and publishers are most grateful for permission to reproduce the following Illustrations which are © copyright of the organisations or individuals listed:

Key
(PC) = Postcard
L = Left – from top down, then base panel L-R
R = Right – from top down, then base panel L-R
(WU)=whereabouts unknown

Illustrations reproduced by permission of the following:
Bristol Central Reference Library (BCRL)
Collage. P5L-R 5 as P12; L-R (5) as P12 L2; L-R (11) as P24 L2; P23 R2; P11 R2;P1 2L2; P 18 L4; P20 L1; P21 R2; P22 L4; P23 R2; P24 L2; P32 L1; P34 L1; P 36 L3; P 40 L4

Answer 20
Queen Victoria's. This is how she looked when she was young. The square was named after her. Would you like a square named after you?

BCRL Newspaper Archives
P38 (Base)

Copyright Bristol City Museums Galleries and Archives (BMAG)
Collage L-R (7) detail from P6-7; P6-7; P 20 L2; P30 L1 detail from P6-7; P41 R1, R2 detail from P6-7

The Clifton Suspension Bridge Trust P29R2

The Science and Society Picture Library Science Museum, London P13R1

The ss Great Britain Trust P29 R1 (Original WU)

John Sansom. Redcliffe Press, Bristol
Collage P5.L-R1 as P28 L2 Passenger Train on Mardyke Quay(photograph) (SU) From *On the Waterfront-The Hotwells Story* by Helen Reid and Sue Stops 2002

Trevor Haddrell
P8-9 (By kind permission of the artist)... exactly as he requested!

The Denise Vincent Archive
P28L2

From private collections
P15 (Base); P17 R2; P21R1 (PC); P23 R1; P25 R1 (PC); P26 L2

Julia Killingback Illustrations
P13 A3, A4; P23 Base; P25 Base; P30 A10, A11; P36 A15

Front & Inside Front Cover
Julia Killingback

Back Cover
Clifton Hill from Sea Banks c 1786 by Nicholas Pocock BMAG

Bristol Mayor George Ferguson
Back cover image of Mayor George Ferguson
The Post www.thisisbristol.co.uk

Wallace & Gromit's Grand Appeal Bristol Children's Hospital Charity Donate (www.grandappeal.org.uk/donate)

Every effort has been made to trace and acknowledge the source of all illustrations included. We would like to apologise for any errors or omissions.

Organisations
The Clifton and Hotwells Improvement Society.

HCCA Hotwells and Cliftonwood Community Association.

Photographs
Most photographs were taken by Julia Killingback and Trevor Palmer. Our thanks are due to Trevor, also to James Barke, and Gary Thoburn.

All images are copyright of the photographers unless otherwise stated.

Series design concept, map and drawn illustrations
© Julia Killingback

Useful contacts
Bristol Ferry Boats
Tel:0117 9273416
www.bristolferry.com

Number Seven Boat Trips
Tel:9293659/07976 554024
www.numbersevenboattrips.com

Avon Gorge and Wildlife Project:
www.avongorge.org.uk

Bristol Central Library:
www.bristol.gov.uk/libraries

Bristol City Museums and Art Galleries:
www.bristol.co.uk/museumsandgalleries

Clifton and Hotwells Improvement Society:
www.cliftonhotwells.org.uk

Clifton Suspension Bridge:
www.cliftonbridge.org.uk

ss Great Britain Trust
www.ss greatbritain.org
Tel: 0117 9260680

Hotwells and Cliftonwood Community Association
www.hotwellscliftonwood.org.uk

Bus information:
www.firstgroup.com/ukbus/bristol_bath

Open Top Bus:
www.citysightseeingbristol.co.uk

Tourist Information:
www.visitbristol.co.uk

Support funding for this project was kindly provided by Bristol City Council Neighbourhood Partnership Well Being Fund

First published 2014
by Julia Killingback
Explorewalks UK
All rights reserved.
Printed by Short Run Press, Exeter
ISBN 978-1-910089-05-7

EXPL◉REWALKS UK
An imprint of Tangent Books
Web orders:
www.explorewalks.co.uk

For our families with love — and for all who delight in taking a step out of the ordinary
JK & MP

3. CLIFTONWOOD

Explore
Bristol

EXPL◉REWALKS UK

ON FOOT

Other Explorewalks titles in the series

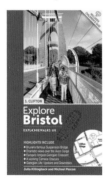

No 1. Clifton

No 2. Victorian Clifton

No 4. Hotwells

For information on other walks
guides in this series go to
www.explorewalks.co.uk